EXTREME DINOSAURS

WORLD'S WEIRDEST DINOSAURS

Rupert Matthews

Raintree

www.raintreepublishers.co.uk

Visit our website to find out more information about Raintree books.

To order:

☎ Phone 0845 6044371

🖨 Fax +44 (0) 1865 312263

✉ Email myorders@raintreepublishers.co.uk

Customers from outside the UK please telephone +44 1865 312262

Raintree is an imprint of **Capstone Global Library Limited**, a company incorporated in England and Wales having its registered office at 7 Pilgrim Street, London, EC4V 6LB – Registered company number: 6695582

Edited by Rebecca Rissman and Laura Knowles
Designed by Richard Parker
Picture research by Mica Brancic
Originated by Capstone Global Library Ltd
Printed and bound in China by CTPS

ISBN 978 1 406 23466 4 (hardback)
15 14 13 12 11
10 9 8 7 6 5 4 3 2 1

ISBN 978 1 406 23473 2 (paperback)
16 15 14 13 12
10 9 8 7 6 5 4 3 2 1

British Library Cataloguing in Publication Data
Matthews, Rupert.
World's weirdest dinosaurs. -- (Extreme dinosaurs)
567.9-dc22
A full catalogue record for this book is available from the British Library.

Acknowledgements
We would like to thank the following for permission to reproduce images: © Capstone Publishers pp. 4-5 (James Field), **6** (Steve Weston), **7** (James Field), **8** (James Field), **9** (Steve Weston), **10** (Steve Weston), **11** (Steve Weston), **12** (Steve Weston), **13** (Steve Weston), **14** (Steve Weston), **15** (Steve Weston), **17** (James Field), **19** (James Field), **20** (Steve Weston), **21** (James Field), **22** (James Field), **23** (Steve Weston), **24** (James Field), **25** (Steve Weston), **26** (Steve Weston); © Miles Kelly Publishing p. **27** (Chris Buzer); Shutterstock p. **29** (© Jorg Hackemann).

Background design features reproduced with permission of Shutterstock/© Szefei/© Fedorov Oleksiy/© Oleg Golovnev/© Nuttakit.

Cover image of an *Incisivosaurus* reproduced with permission of © Capstone Publishers/James Field.

We would like to thank Nathan Smith for his invaluable help in the preparation of this book.

Every effort has been made to contact copyright holders of material reproduced in this book. Any omissions will be rectified in subsequent printings if notice is given to the publishers.

Contents

Some words are shown in bold, **like this**. You can find out what they mean by looking in the glossary.

Weird and wonderful

Dinosaurs were a group of animals that lived millions of years ago. Some of them were really weird. They had horns, crests, or frills. Some found food in peculiar ways. Others may have behaved in odd ways. They were all very different from modern animals.

Did you know?
Dinosaurs lived in a time
known as the **Mesozoic Era.**

5

The clawed arm

The arms of *Patagonykus* were short and strong. Each arm ended in a single curved claw that could rip and tear. *Patagonykus* must have had trouble picking things up! It is thought that *Patagonykus* may have ripped open termite nests with its claws and then licked up the insects with a long tongue. Yum!

Did you know?
Patagonykus's jaws were long and thin but it only had a few teeth.

Triple claws

Therizinosaurus was nearly 10 metres long. That is as long as three cows end to end. Each hand had three huge claws. The longest claw was longer than your entire arm! Some scientists think it used the claws to pull down tree branches. It could then eat the leaves and twigs. Other scientists think it used the claws to dig in the ground. It may have fed on roots or insects.

Therizinosaurus

claws

Domed skulls

The bone head **dinosaurs** had the thickest skull bones of any animal ever! *Stegoceras* had a **dome** of bone nearly 8 centimetres thick on top of its skull. *Stygimoloch* had a smaller skull dome, but it did have curved spikes. The longest spike was at least 10 centimetres long. That's nearly as long as a pen. Both these dinosaurs were about the size of a sheep.

Stegoceras

Stygimoloch

Horned hunter

Carnotaurus was a big hunting **dinosaur**. It was almost as large as an elephant but had tiny front legs. *Carnotaurus* had two stout horns on its head, just like a bull. It may have used these for fighting. Although it was big and tough, its jaws were thin and weak. Nobody knows how *Carnotaurus* moved around, or hunted, because it didn't even have claws!

horns

13

Weird sauropods

Sauropod dinosaurs were huge plant-eaters that walked on all four legs. Most sauropods had long tails, long necks, and small heads. *Agustinia* had spikes growing from its neck, back, and tail. These were probably used as protection against hunters.

spike

Agustinia

Did you know?
Brachytrachelopan was a sauropod with a short neck. Its neck was less than half the size of other sauropod necks.

Brachytrachelopan

Humpback

The plant-eater *Ouranosaurus* was about three times bigger than a rhinoceros. It lived in a dry area of Africa where plants grew for only a few months each year. Along the back of *Ouranosaurus* was a line of tall bones. These supported a flap of skin. When food was easy to find, *Ouranosaurus* may have stored fat in the flap so that it could survive when food was difficult to find. Camels do the same today.

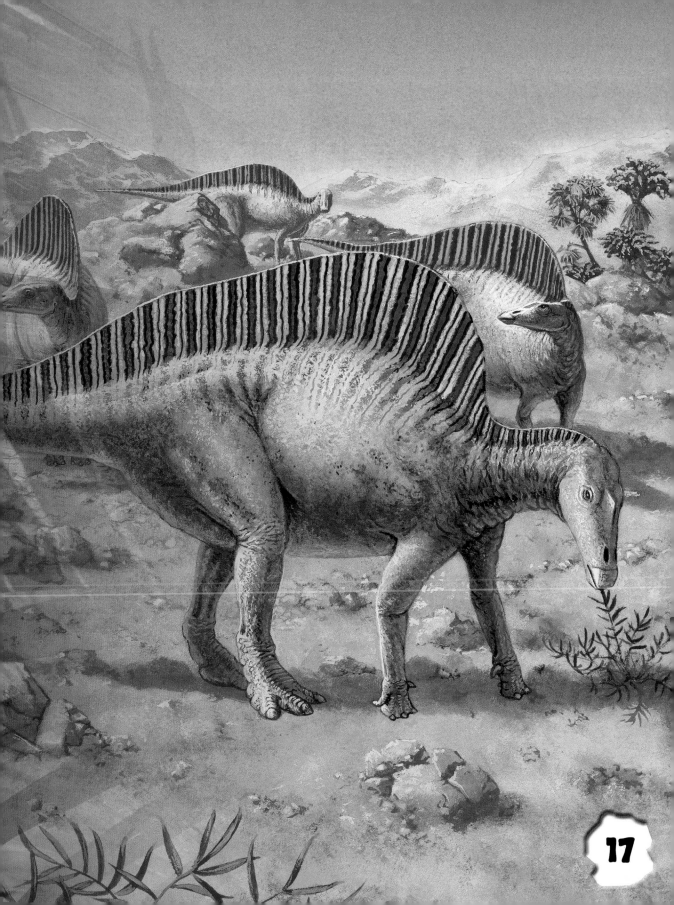

The crested killer

The hunter *Cryolophosaurus* grew to be nearly 8 metres long. That is nearly as long as two cars. It had strong claws on its arms and powerful jaws. On top of its head was a crest of bone that ran from side to side above the eyes. Perhaps the crest was brightly coloured to make the **dinosaur's** head look bigger from the front. That would not only look weird but would scare other animals too!

Horned dinosaurs

The **ceratopsian dinosaurs** were plant-eaters that had horns and neck shields. *Pachyrhinosaurus* had two curved horns growing from the top of its shield. Where all other horned dinosaurs had a horn on their nose, *Pachyrhinosaurus* had a weird lump of bone instead. It was a strange-looking dinosaur!

Crested duckbills

The plant-eating **hadrosaur dinosaurs** had a wide variety of crests on top of their heads. The crests were probably brightly coloured. *Olorotitan* had a fan-shaped crest that pointed backwards. *Charonosaurus* had a long, tube-shaped crest. The crest may have been joined to the neck with a large flap of coloured skin. It would have waved this like a fan to impress other dinosaurs.

Olorotitan

Did you know?
The only part of *Charonosaurus* that scientists have ever found is its head.

Charonosaurus

Deadly tails

Some **dinosaurs** had a deadly weapon on their tail – spikes! *Shunosaurus* was a **sauropod** that grew to be about 10 metres long. It had a spiked bone club on the end of its tail. *Wuerhosaurus* was a **stegosaurid** that was 6 metres long, a bit longer than a car. It had short, stumpy legs while other stegosaurs had longer legs.

Shunosaurus

Wuerhosaurus

Ankylosaurus

Ankylosaurus was an armoured **dinosaur** that grew to be 9 metres long. That is almost as long as a bus! It was covered in **armour** made of bone and horn. The armour ran in bands from one side of the body to the other. The skull was covered in bone armour, as was the tail. The only part of the dinosaur not covered in armour was its belly.

Visiting a museum

The **dinosaurs** shown in this book are not alive any more today. You can see **fossils** of dinosaurs at museums. These fossils are usually bones and teeth. The fossils will have signs next to them explaining what they are. Before visiting a museum look at their website or phone them to see if they have any dinosaur displays.

CITY PASS
VOUCHERS

29

Glossary

armour outer shell or bone on some dinosaurs that protected their bodies

ceratopsian describes a family of horned plant-eating dinosaurs that lived in North America and Asia towards the end of the age of dinosaurs

dinosaur group of animals that lived on land millions of years ago during the Mesozoic Era

dome rounded shape

fossil part of a plant or animal that has been buried in rocks for millions of years

hadrosaurs family of plant-eating dinosaurs. They are also known as duckbills because many of them had wide, flat mouths that looked like the bill of a duck.

Mesozoic Era part of Earth's history that is sometimes called the "Age of Dinosaurs". It is divided into three periods: Triassic, Jurassic, and Cretaceous.

sauropod family of plant-eating dinosaurs that had long necks and long tails. The largest dinosaurs of all were sauropods.

stegosaurid group of plant-eating dinosaurs that had spikes or plates of bone sticking out of their backs and tails

Find out more

Books

Dinosaur Dig (series), Rupert Matthews (QED, 2009)
Explorers: Dinosaurs, Dougal Dixon (Kingfisher, 2010)
First Encyclopedia of Dinosaurs and Prehistoric Life,
    Sam Taplin (Usborne, 2011)
Who Cleans Dinosaur Bones?: Working at a Museum
    (Wild Work), Margie Markarian (Raintree, 2010)

Websites

www.dinosaurden.co.uk
Information about dinosaurs, as well as puzzles and games can
be found on this site.

www.kidsdinos.com
This fun website has games as well as information about
dinosaurs.

www.nhm.ac.uk/kids-only/dinosaurs
The Natural History Museum's website has lots of information
about dinosaurs, including facts, quizzes, and games.

www.thedinosaurmuseum.com/html/dinosaur-facts.html
Find out more about dinosaurs on the Dinosaur Museum website.

Index